Anonymous

Principles of the Roman, Protestant and Christian Churches

Anonymous

Principles of the Roman, Protestant and Christian Churches

ISBN/EAN: 9783337044220

Printed in Europe, USA, Canada, Australia, Japan

Cover: Foto ©Lupo / pixelio.de

More available books at **www.hansebooks.com**

PRINCIPLES

OF THE

ROMAN, PROTESTANT

AND

CHRISTIAN CHURCHES

.

.

FLORENCE

CLAUDIAN PRESS

—

1864.

PREFACE

These three historical dissertations form the introduction to a new Edition of Plymouthist tracts, which have for years past been industriously circulated among the infant Churches of Italy.

The work is published under the title of " Principles of the Romish, Protestant and Christian Churches, " and is attributed, on good authority, to the pens of Messrs Magrini and Rossetti and Count Guicciardini.

Much has already been written in the pages of "Christian Work," "Evangelical Christendom" and other journals with regard to the scandal created among the Christians of Italy last winter by the appearance of this work, and doubtless much yet remains to be written.

Several of the Free Italian Churches have protested, while others have silently acquiesced.

The whole controversy which has arisen hinges on the fact that, altho published anonymously, the work was issued in the name of the Free Italian Churches. Those of them therefore which have refused to protest have been justly held to accept the views expounded in their name. This is denied, of course, by some of their friends, but all who are acquainted with the opinions of these non-protesting churches, know it to be a fact that they do sympathize with these Plymouthist principles, as one or two of them have been forward to publish.

The Free Italian Church in Genoa refused, at the suggestion of Signor Mazzarella, to protest, so that D.ʳ Desanctis and others have lately withdrawn from the communion of the Free Italian Churches, under the solemn conviction that they are " infected with Plymouthism. "

The accompanying translation of the anonymous " Introduction " has been printed, in order to acquaint the English public as to the true state of the case. Christians at home are not aware, in many instances, of what they are supporting when they contribute to the " Gospel in Italy, " and they will thus have an opportunity of judging for themselves, and acting upon the decision of their Christian manhood and their common sense.

The translation, which is a faithful one, has not been easily accomplished, owing to the state of the original, which, in the judgement of those most capable of deciding, is in bad Italian, and pays little regard to punctuation or the ordinary rules of composition.

Florence, September 1864.

CHAPTER I.

THE ROMISH CHURCH.

Exalted wisdom and power of arms did not give to
Greece the duration desired by her founders: she fell
through her false civilization and became a province of
the Roman empire. Thereupon the science of Greece
was wedded to that of Rome, their systems of religion
became more intimately united, and everyone believed
that by knowledge and by the sword the Roman empire
was to endure for ever. But the mythological religion
of the Greeks and the Latins, giving them vices and superstitions, and exciting them to violence and treachery,
corrupted them, threw them into atheism — and first the
Western, then the Eastern Empire became an easy prey
to barbarians.

Even from the times of Augustus mythological
religion, despised by all, was declining, and wise men
were seeking to know and possess the Truth. This desire
was inspired by God himself, whilst he who was, and
is, and ever shall be *the eternal Truth* was descending

from the Father, and to that generation, lost in error and dead in sins, was exclaiming: *I am the Way, the Truth and the Life* (John xiv, 6).

Then men were panting after a future life, and thronged the academies to receive it from the Platonists, who discoursed of the life to come without knowing where or what it was. And the Gospel sounded forth in those halls the memorable words of John: *in Christ is the life, and the life is the light of men* (John. 1. 4).

Then all had an excellent opinion of themselves and believed themselves honest, wise, just, true, but God showed them that *all men have sinned and have come short of the glory of God* (Rom. iii, 23).

Convinced of sin they endeavored to free their souls from it, but the Gospel came quickly to proclaim in the depths of the soul the words of the Baptist, *Behold the Lamb of God* (Christ) *which taketh away the sin of the world* (John i, 29). *What must I do to be saved?* exclaimed then the sinner, and the disciples of the Redeemer answered: *Believe in the Lord Jesus Christ, and thou shalt be saved, and all thy house* (Acts xvi, 30, 31). And truly *Jesus*, who is *God manifest in the flesh* (1 Tim. iii, 16), has taken away sin in his body on the cross, and has cancelled it from the Father's presence with his blood; therefore whosoever receives that blood has remission of his sins, cleansing from them and eternal life (Col. i, 14; ii, 11, 14).

Yes. He gave Himself for us, died for us, was buried and now c sits at the right hand of the majesty (Heb. i, 3), Mediator between God and man (1 Tim. ii, 5), propitiation for our sins » (1 John ii, 2).

Christ commanded to preach salvation by grace
through faith (Eph. ii, 8, 9; Rom. v, 1, 2) first, the
Apostles (Matt. x, 1, 7: Mark iii, 13, 14: vi, 7;
Luke ix, 1, 2), then, the disciples (Luke x, 1, 16).

He willed that believers, (not the world) should ce-
lebrate the supper, remembering that He died for them
in remission of sins (Matt. xxvi, 26, 29. Mark xiv,
22, 25. Luke xx, 19, 20), and should do this until
He come again (1 Cor. xi, 26). He commanded the
Gospel to be preached, and that they who believed should
be baptized to show that they were dead to sin and
risen again to a new life. (Matt. xxviii, 18, 28. Mark
xvi, 15, 20. Luke xxiv, 50, 53. Rom. vi, 1, 6. Col.
ii, 12, 14; 1 Peter iii, 21).

These are the vital doctrines of the Gospel taught
and practised by the Apostles and by the Disciples.
But Italy retained for a short time, like every other
country, the purity of the Gospel (and the doctrines
of the Apostles), since even after the time of Paul the
Church was already unfaithful and in the 3rd century
had many strange doctrines. Let us examine that
which happened *after the death of the Apostles.*

II.

OF THE ROMAN CATHOLICS, AND OF THEIR INVENTION
OF DOCTRINES AND FORMS TO ABOLISH THE SUPPER
AND TO ESTABLISH THE MASS.

Without following the history of all the heresies ori-
ginated by those who were not willing to keep faith-

fully and strictly close to the Word of God, let us see that which has led to the present state of religious principle in Italy. In the apostolic times, and in the first centuries of Christianity *Roman Catholics* were not known, but little by little arose this apostasy which has arrived, as in the present time, at denying Christ to be the Saviour, pretending that man may save himself by his own merits and by his own works. The doctrines and the forms of Romanism are certainly not found in the Bible; sometimes it retains the names of the truths, but the meaning which it attributes to them is false, and therefore confuses the understanding and the conscience of whoever follows it. Thus the different bishops and popes of Rome have added in different centuries the doctrines and the forms which follow, in order to abolish the Holy supper and to establish in its stead the Mass.

When the faithful were gathered together for public worship and to break bread (1 Cor. xiv, 25), two or three prophets spake and the others judged (ib. 29), and the Romanists make all be silent that the priest alone may speak. Then one gave a psalm, another gave doctrine (ib. 25), now the priest gives out everything. Then there was the spirit of prayer (Rom. viii, 26) but it was soon extinguished by those who were « lords over » the flock of God, and *written prayers, liturgies* and the « *oremus* » were introduced. At first the cup was taken with simplicity and in glass vessels, but in the third century they began to think that the appearance of shining things was. worth much in the eyes of God, and Urban I introduced chalices of *pewter*, and then of *silver*. At first,

the ministers dressed like every one else, as did Jesus
Christ, the Apostles and the disciples, but in that
same century Stephen I invented the *priest's dress*, and
the moveable table on which were placed the bread
and the wine was covered with a splendid *cloth*. Sixtus II went further, and treating that table as a sacred thing, ordered that the psalms and chants should
he snng before those pieces of wood joined together.
They began to speak of the *altar*. Mark ordered that
after the reading of a chapter in the Gospel, *the Ni-
cene creed*, composed by Osio, bishop of Cordova,
should be sung by the people and the Clergy.

In the IV century, Liberius prohibited the communion, 1stly to the uninstructed catechumens, 2dly to unab-
solved penitents, 3rdly to demoniacs, who were all dis-
missed with the words: *ite missa est*, whence comes
the word *Mass*. Damaso added the *Gloria Patri* and
the *Confiteor*. Anastasius ordered the fasting before the
communion, forgetting that Jesus and the Apostles ate
before the Holy Supper, (Luke XXII, 14, 20) and so also
did the Corinthians (1 Cor. XI).

In the 5th century Celestinus I ordered that the psalms
should be sung by the assembly during the mass,
and that the priest who was celebrating it should en-
circle himself with the mistery of words murmured
sotto voce. He afterwards had the *introito*, the *graduali*
and the *offertorii* composed, and gave rules for the communion.

In the 6th century Gregory I, called the Great, introduced the *ceremonies* and the *genuflections*, invented
other *oremus*, arranged the *introito* better, instituted

the *Kyrie eleison* to be repeated nine times, the *alleluia*, the *Deus in adjutorium*, and the *requiescat in pace*. Indeed he arranged the mass in the way in which it is now said, but transubstantiation and the adoration of the host were wanting. He abolished preaching before the mass, because of the gross ignorance of the priests and the bishops, who did not even know how to read correctly.

In the 7th century, under Agathom, and at the meeting of the Council of Constantinople, held in 650, John bishop of Porto, celebrated the first *mass in latin*, without mixing therein anything of the vulgar tongue.

In the 8th century, the masses were still celebrated in the meetings or assemblies of the catholics, and it was not yet known that four fine walls ought to be called church or temple.

The priests, taking advantage in that century of the ignorance of the people, instituted private *masses*. The loaf of the Supper was replaced by a *wafer*, or *host* as it is called, and the large vessels of wine by *ampolline* (small phials). The people were angry, and no longer brought gifts to the priests, but the latter to reingratiate themselves gave them back the loaf of the communion. In those times, the priests recited aloud the words of the supper, but later they murmured them between their teeth to give an air of mystery. In this same century, Gregory II having obtained many pagan temples, changed them into *churches*, and perverted the sense of this word, which signifies *assembly of the faithful* (Matt. xviii. 17: 1 Cor. i, 2, etc.) and *Body of Christ* (Eph. i, 22, 23); afterwards he ordained that the mass should be recited in in those temples. Leo III added the *smoke of the censers*. And finally, in that century, the first fables which were to serve for the dogma of transubstantiation began to be spread abroad. A monk said that he had seen Jesus Christ in the form of a child on the communion table; another friar asserted that Witikind, king of Saxony, having gone into church, set himself to observe the method used by the faithful in the communion, when lo! he saw go into their mouths a smiling and graceful child: — and there were those who said they had seen the host shed blood, and those who had seen a child whom the angels held on the altar and then cut into little bits — and other impious and wicked puerilities. Pascasius, bishop of Corbey in Saxony, took possession of these fables and invented transubstantiation, but popes, archbishops and bishops opposed it.... and afterwards admitted its strange dogma!

In the 9th century, Sergius III added to the mass the *breaking of the wafer into three parts*. In the 11th, under Clement Ist, the priest gave to the said wafer the high title of sacrament of the altar, and under Leo 9th, in the Council of « Laterano », transubstantiation was admitted, whilst St. Augustin had said « that the sacred « body of Jesus Christ was as far from the sacrament « as the highest heaven is distant from the earth. » In the 12th, were instituted *masses in honor of the saints*, and they were known as *great, small, high, low, dry, hurried, etc.*

Then, under Innocent III the portable tables became *altars* and were *consecrated*. In the 13th century, Honorius III ordained that the *host should be worshipped*.

But with all these innovations there was much anarchy among the priests, and in the different churches, and there was no uniformity in the manner of saying mass. In some of them, the cup was still given to the communicants, until in the Council of Constance, opened in in 1415, it was taken away, and reserved for the priests only. Hear the decree of the 13th session of that Council.

« Although Jesus Christ after supper instituted and administered to his disciples this venerable sacrament in both kinds, (bread and wine) notwithstanding this the authorities of the Holy Canons(?) and the commendable custom of the Church (?) have ordered and still order that it should not be administered after supper, nor should be taken by those who have already eaten, excepting the sick. And although in the primitive Church this sacrament was distributed to the faithful in both kinds, nevertheless to avoid certain dangers, (?) and scandals, (?) another custom was reasonably introduced, in which they who consecrate communicate in both kinds, and laymen in that of bread only, believing always and firmly, without doubting it in any way, that the body and blood of Christ are wholly contained in the « Kind » – bread, and in the other, wine. Therefore is to be reputed heretical the opinion of those who hold this usage as sacrilegious and unlawful, and they who obstinately maintain the communion in both kinds are to be reproved as heretics, and even with this present edict we order all parish priests and inquisitors to punish such heretics severely ».

— *Item :* « We forbid all priests to administer to lay-

men this sacrament in both kinds, under penalty of ex-
communnication. » — The chancellor Gerson (*Tract.
contr. hacres de com. sub. utr spec.*) has left us the list
of the reasons for which the Council *prohibited the cup:*
1st the beard, which grows long and covers the chin and
the lips; 2nd the dislike which many persons have to
drinking from the same cup; 3rd the expense of buying
wine; 4th the frost, in winter; 5th the flies, in summer;
6th the embarrassment of the deacons in administering
the cup to the faithful; 7th the danger of spilling any
on the ground: 8th finally, the unworthy state of the
people who ought not to resemble the priests in the act
of communion. — But had not *Jesus* Christ said *Drink
ye all of it?* (Matt. xxvi, 27).

This then is how the Holy Supper of the Lord, adul-
terated in form, in substance and in application, was
replaced by a *wafer, and the worship in spirit and in
truth of all the faithful* was reduced to a crowd of silent
people gaping behind a priest, who mutters between
his teeth a mass invented and managed by him. Is this
religion a Christian one?

III.

OF OTHER INVENTIONS OF CEREMONIES AND DOGMAS.

We have seen how the adoration of God in spirit and
truth became a carnal worship of visible things; and all
that pleases the eye, that delights the ear and flatters
the heart, which over loves what is material, replaced the
Gospel. The Romish priests, once on the slope of error,

slipped irrecoverably on and never rose again. Their inventions were multiplied. They wished to accommodate
the pagans in order to make them become Romanists,
and gave a Gospel tint to all tho superstitions of the
idolaters.

The 'latter had a *basin* and the *sprinkling brush* near
the doors of their temples, and they who entered received that purifying water: — and Alexander 1, who was
popo in 120, replaced the custom by a so-called *holy water.* But of one water alone the Gospel speaks, and of that
wo all have need — of that which flows from the side
of Christ. (John xix. 34: 1 John v, 6).

Urban I in the 3ᵈ century introduced the *Chrism* or
confirmation after baptism, while the Gospel says that
it is the Holy Spirit who seals and confirms in us the
work of Christ. (Eph. 1 13; 2 Cor. 1 22; Luke xxiv,
48, 49; Acts ii, 33 etc). And in that century they began
to *pray for the dead*, because they believed that the souls
of the faithful were to enjoy the presence of God after
the day of judgement. See the contrary, Phil I, 23;
Luke xxiii, 43.

In tho 4ᵗʰ century under, Silvestro I, *candles* were introduced, just as if He who created the Sun and the Stars
(Gen. 1, 16) requires such wretched little light to see
by ! Had He not said, *I am the Light of the World ?*
(John viii, 12) — At that time several lazy people,
guided by Basilius, in order to lead an idle and glutton-
ous life, instituted *monachism*: thus they pretended to
take themselves away from the world: see the contrary, John xvii, 15. — They instituted *feasts in honor
of the Saints* beginning by that of *St. Peter in Fetters;*

but St. Peter himself will reprove them in the day of judgement; Acts x, 25 26. — At this time they even established the *worship of the relics of martyrs* to oppose the worship of their dead by the pagans: see the contrary, Job xv, 14-16. Pope Sergius introduced *plaster images*: see the contrary, Exod xxiii, 54; xx, 3-5.

In the 5th century, the papists having become deaf and not frequenting the churches, were called there like the Druids, by the *sound of bells* purposely invented: Sixtus III endowed the Church with *chaplets*, *candlesticks* and *censers*, all Jewish things, against which Paul wrote; (see the Epist. to Galatians); Leo I invented *the litanies*, read the contrary, Matt. vi, 7, 8; and then the processions of the *Catholic idols*, according to the custom of the pagans and the Buddhists. — Pope Hilarius with the *exorcisms* and *the processions of the saints* pretended to drive away the devil, but Christ alone can do this work (1 John iii, 8) — Felix III *consecrated the churches*, for then as we have before said, the Church was no longer the meeting of the faithful, nor the Body of Christ, but four walls.

In the 6th century, Gregory I on the authority of Plato, of Cicero and of Virgil proved the existence of Purgatory !!! Who would have thought that Plato, Cicero and Virgil were fathers of the Romish Church! But so says Bellarmin (De Purgat. L, i, cap. 11). Our purgatory (purification) is Christ. (1 John ii, 2: Mat xxv, 11, 12, 46; Luke xxiii, 43).

In the 7th century, Vitalianus, to tickle and charm the ears of the Catholics, introduced *organs in the Churches*, but the Lord wishes us to sing *with the heart* and not with *the organ* (Eph. v, 19: Col iii 16). And in this century, tho pope, becomo a demigod, introduced the *Kissing of the feet:* this Jesus never did, see John xiii, 4-10; — and grasped at a littlo temporal power; see tho contrary in John xviii, 37.

In tho 8th century Leo III introduced the use of *incense*, but the Word speaks of another perfume, Phil. iv, 18, 2 Cor ii, 15.

In the 9th century Leo IV instituted fasting on *Friday* and *Saturday*, and thus meat which was pure and holy from Sunday to Thursday was declared impure on Friday and Saturday ! (See tho contrary in Matt. xv, 11; Mark vii. 15; Acts xi, 9; Rom xiv, 17; 1 Cor x, 25, 26, Col. ii 16, 20, 25; 1 Tim iv, 1-5) — In this century also *saints were canonized* and *bells baptized !*

In tho 10th were invented tho *holy water brush* and the *consecration of the priests.* Then came *indulgences;* but it is the blood of Jesus Christ which cleanses us from all sin (1 John i, 7); and Jesus does not give us indulgence in order that we may sin (see I John iii, 8).

In the 13th century the Inquisition was invented, which laid waste and slaughtered Albigenses, Cattari etc. (See the contrary: Luke ix, 54, 56). The statistics of this horrible massacre are not known, but wo have the numbers of the slaughtered in Spain from 1481 to 1801, from which it appears that 34,658 were burnt alive; 18,049 burnt in effigy; 288,214 imprisoned with confiscation of their goods; and all this independently of the massacres of the Huguenots, etc. But as a compensation Alano della Rupe invented the *rosary*, which

is quite a pastime and rather profane, for one can say
one's beads walking, sitting and doing any thing (see
the contrary, Matt. VI, 7, 8).

And finally, in the midst of the 19ᵗʰ century, Pius
IX has declared that Mary was conceived without sin,
although in the Magnificat Mary owns herself to be a
sinner and exclaims: « Et exultavit spiritus meus in
Deo *salutari meo* » (Luke I. 47) and St. Paul says that
all are born in sin (Rom. v, 12, 18: XI, 32).

IV.

INVENTION OF THE DRESS AND THE TITLES
FOR THE POPE AND THE PRIEST.

With such profanations and adulterations of the Christian dogma, the ministers became the lords of the
Church, introduced the distinctions of clergy and laymen (see the contrary Gal III, 27-29: Rom. x, 12:
1 Cor. XII, 13; Col. III, 11), and changed dresses, customs and names.

In the 2ⁿᵈ century Telesphorus assumed the name of
Pope or Father in the second Decretal (see the contrary
Matt. XXIII, 9), and in the same century Pope Anicetus
(forgetting that Christ, the Apostles and all the primitive Christians dressed in the ordinary, universal manner, and wore beards and hair (as they themselves re-
present them in their pictures) prohibited the priests'
wearing a beard, and ordered that they should have a
shaven crown. In the 4ᵗʰ century, Sylvester I invented
the tunic and the alb (see the contrary Matt XXIII, 5);

Mark called himself *Universal bishop,* (while the Apostle
Peter called himself *bishop among the bishops* (1 Pet.
v. 1.) and introduced the « Pallium » for the bishops.
Sergius prohibited the *marriage of the priests,* showing
the vii chap. to the Romans, v. 3, whilst St. Paul says
that the Bishop should be the husband of one wife, as
also the deacons(1 Tim. iii, 1-11).But every one laugh-
ed at this law till 950; since Bonifacius I, Felix III,
and. Gelasius I, popes, were *sons of priests.* Sergius,
seeing that the emperor Gratianus had renounced the
title of *Sovereign Pontiff* or Head of the Augurs took it
for himself! (see the contrary Heb. iv, 14). In the 6th
century, Gregory I, to preserve the property of the
Church and not to give it any longer to the sons of the
priests, instituted *celibacy,* (see the contrary 1 Tim,
iv, 1-3). In the 6th century, John V encircled his head
with the *mitred crown,* (see the contrary in John xviii,
36). Sergius II ordained that his *feet should be kissed*
(see contrary in John xiii, 4-15,) and in the 8th century,
Zachary ordered that the priests should wear in the
church, *cloaks adorned with gold and jewels,* leaving off
the true vestments which are read of in Col iii, 12.
Eventually the popes made themselves *lords of the world*
and *distributors* of *Kingdoms,* receiving such power from
quite another than God! Read Luke iv, 6.

V.

So that in the present century Romanism has arrived, among many errors of doctrines and of forms:

1st At adulterating the holy Supper:

a) In the form: no longer *bread and wine* (Matt. xxvi, 26-90, etc) but a wafer; and denies the cup to the people.

b) In the *substance*: no longer the *remembrance* of the death of Christ, (I Cor. xi, 24, 25), but a fresh death inflicted upon the Lord, against that which St. Paul says. (Heb. x, 24; vi, 6).

c) In the *application*: no longer to the *faithful* (Matt. xxvi, 26-28; 1 Cor. x, 20, 21), but to all, including the wordlings of its Church.

2. At *baptizing infants*, and at pretending to make them Christians when they have not first believed: « He that *believeth* and is baptized shall be saved, » saith the Lord. (Mark xvi, 16).

3. At inventing *purgatory*, while in the Word it is said that Jesus Christ is the « propitiation for our sins» and not an imaginary fire ! (1 John ii, 2; Matt. xxv, 11, 12, 46; Luke xxiii, 43).

4. At causing *saints* and *angels* to be adored; (see the contrary, Acts x, 25, 26; xiv, 14, 15; Col. ii, 18; Rev. xix, 10; xxii, 8, 9).

5. At making the saints in heaven *intercede* for us, when they are unable to do anything for us. (Phil, iv, 6; Heb. iv, 13-16; vii, 25; Is xliv, 9-20; Ps. cx; 2 Thes.

III, 10; John xvi, 23; 1 Tim ii, 5; 1 John ii, 1, 2; 2 Tim. iii).

6. At preaching *salvation by works;* (see against this Matt. xix, 25, 26; Luke xvii, 10; John vi, 28, 29; Rom. iii, 10, 27; Gal. ii, 16; iii, 10, 11; v, 4; Eph. ii, 1, 8. 9).

7. At making us *pray for the dead;* (see Gal. vi, 5; 1 Thes. iv, 13. 14; v, 9; 1 Tim ii, 5, 6; 1 Cor. iv, 5; vii, 23; Titus iii, 5).

8. At making us worship Mary; (see the contrary Matt. xii; 48-50; Mark iii, 33-35; Luke 1. 30, 46-50; ii, 48, 49; vii, 20-21; xi, 27, 28; John ii, 4; xix, 26).

9. At *prohibiting meats* on certain days; (see the contrary Matt. xv, 11; Mark. vii, 15; Acts xi, 9 Rom. xiv, 17; 1 Cor. x, 25 26; Col. ii, 16-25; 1 Tim iv, 1-3).

10. At *forbidding the marriage of priests;* (see the contrary in Matt viii, 14; 1 Cor. vii, 9. ix, 5; 1 Tim iii, 2-18; iv, 1-3; Titus 1, 5-6):

11. At saying that *infants dying unbaptized are lost;* (see the contrary in Matt. xix, 14, Mark x, 14; Luke xviii, 16).

12. At prohibiting the reading of the Bible; (see the contrary in Luke xvi, 29, 31; John v, 39-47, xii, 48; Act xvii, 11; Eph. vi, 17; Col. iv, 15; 1 Thess. v, 27; 2 Tim. iii, 16; Heb. iv, 12; Rev. i, 3; xiv, 6; xxii, 19).

13. At substituting for the Bible the *traditions and doctrines of men;* (see the contrary Matt. xv, 3-9 Mark vii, 7-13; Col ii, 8; Rev. xxii, 18).

14. And against the *pretensions of the pope and the clergy,* read Matt. xxiii, 9; John xviii, 36; 1 Cor. iii 11; Gal. i, 8, ii, 11; 2 Thess. ii, 3, 4, 8-10; 1 Peter v, 1-3, etc.

This is the Romish religion to which the superstitious, infidels and knaves are devoted. Without faith, without honesty, it may be called « the mystery of iniquity », introduced into the Church after the death of the Apostles (2 Thess. ɪɪ, 7). Unfaithful to the Word, it uses every effort against it, and hates it, knowing that by the Gospel it is condemned. Compare the passages quoted with its inventions, and you will see that this Church has always worked against the Holy Scriptures. This is why it hates and condemns them, — this is why in these very days its priests have even come to uttering the impious heresy: are you certain that the Bible is the Word of God? — this is why they hate it, and would wish to take it out of the hands of the people, because they know that the Bible disperses the shades of human superstitions, and presents Jesus as the Saviour, the Life, and the Light of all who hear His word, and believe in Him who sent him (John ɪ, 1-9; v, 24).

And then — recall to mind the mournful pages of the history of Romanism, and you will see how that Church has prostituted herself to the powerful ones of the earth in order to tyrannize over the bodies and souls of all nations; — you will see that she has given the saints into the hands of the violent, and thus has caused them to be put to death without pity; — you will see that the blood of the martyrs, sprinkled over her, caused her garments to be scarlet-coloured (Rev: xvɪɪ, 3); — you will see that she has become one body with the world, and is full of violence and fraud — you will see that she has lost all that is heavenly, and therefore has earthly deities, human traditions, and purple on her shoulders, instead of worshipping God in spirit and in truth, preaching the Gospel, and being clothed in the righteousness of Christ. And poor, blind, wretched, naked and miserable as she is; she believes herself rich, and having need of nothing (Rev. III, 17, 18), is arrayed in superb vanity, and fills Italy with blood in order to retain a strip of land. And she yet continues to intrigue with the different powers, and to beg from them such protection as may avail her, having neither celestial strength nor earthly force of her own; still, in her agony, she answers to every demand of the civilized world, *non possumus;* but it is written in the Word (which this church hates) that God will eventually put it into the heart of the reigning ones to execute his sentence against this religion; then they « shall hate her, shall make her desolate and naked, and burn her with fire » (Rev. XVII, 16). This is the final sentence of God against Romanism, and against all religions which are worldly and unfaithful to the Word, — therefore the Protestant religions will have the same fate. This prophecy is already beginning to be fulfilled. Romanism foresees already that those powers which now unwillingly support it, will one day destroy it; — and Protestantism feels that the State by which it has been supported, has eaten into and cankered it; — knows that the popish forms, ceremonies and liturgies which have crept into it, have extinguished its vitality, so that it has an appearance of life, but is in fact a frozen corpse! (Rev. III, 1).

Oh Italians, let him who thirsts for life. go to Him

who is the Life, to Jesus; — let him who would walk
in the light, go to Him who is the Light — let him
who would bo saved, go to the Saviour, to Jesus; —
let him who would be taught go to the Bible, *but to
the Bible only*, the word of Jesus! Courage, then, let
us all go to Jesus!

CHAPTER II.

THE PROTESTANT CHURCH.

I.

THE FIRST PROTESTANTS WERE THE WALDENSES, WHO WERE ORIGINALLY SANDALED FRIARS.

In speaking of the Protestants, who have different confessions of faith, different ministries, and many denominations, we ought to entitle this chapter, the *Protestant Churches*. But as it appears that they all wish to unite in a certain sense in the *Evangelical Alliance*, (with the exception of the congregations of the Brethren) although they still retain their special forms and their names, we will also consider them as one body, and will give them the name of *Protestant Church*.

The Waldenses were the first Protestants who protested against the Church of Rome, therefore we will begin by speaking of them; then of the Churches risen out of the Reformation of the 16th century, down to our own days; reserving the last paragraph of this chapter for the Brethren, who have no connection with the formalist, traditionalist Protestants.

Whilst the Roman Empire was falling the Church was becoming an earthly power. She received the Italians who wished to defend themselves, gave them captains and armed bishops, and they fought; finally, the barbarians being converted to Romanism, made alliance with the pope, who, by the religious ascendancy which he exorcised, found himself all at once the head of a sect, a prince, the dispenser of crowns and the arbiter of kings. Then he endeavoured to establish himself firmly, taking advantage of the dogmas which exercise a strong influence over men, and promulgated them to all Catholics, and amongst others to those who, through the wickedness of the times and through superstition, had chosen a monastic life, and lived retired among the mountains which crown Italy. When it was known that Vigilantius, a Catholic priest in Barcelona, had passed through Lombardy and the Cottian Alps, preaching against the new doctrines (that is, idolatry, celibacy, pilgrimages), and that he had found many listeners, Jerome called him « hydra, cerberus, centaur, agent of the demon » *(Jeron. tom.* II, *p.* 120–126, *et adv. Vig. Op. tom.* I, *p.* 589), and denounced him to the pope. Amongst those who followed the doctrines of Vigilantius may be enumerated the Waldensian monks, inhabitants of the Cottian Alps. And indeed a Catholic bishop. Mg^r Charvaz, (Histoire des Vaudois) believes that they were *bare-footed friars, sabatati or insabatati,* that is, shod with soles or sandals (De Pottor, St. del Crist. § 2). who were not unmarried in those days, as friars are now. They *first* rebelled against the pope in order to continue to marry. This is not a supposition, for if the various

customs and usages practised by the Waldenses np to
our own days aro attentively compared with the customs
and usages of the Romish friars and priests, it will be seen
that we are right. As an example it may snffice to mention
the black gown worn by Waldensian ministers when they
officiato, similar to that used by the primitive bare-
footed friars, and later by the Augustinians, whence tho
black and monastic gown worn afterwards by Lntheran
ministers. Also the *fast on the day of the supper*, as among
the Roman Catholics, and the *form of their temples* similar to that of the pagans. It is known that the
Romanists un-heathenized the temples of Jupiter, of
Apollo, of Venus, and then accommodated them to
their own use, therefore the Waldenses also used the
pagan form for their temples, that is, a large navo
in tho centre, and sometimes with two small side aisles.
Add further the *observance of certain popish festivals;
Easter, Christmas-day, etc.; — the supper on those days,*
like the papists; — *certain Romish expressions in their
liturgy and preaching,* as for example *the confession of
sins,* corresponding to tho « Confiteor », and then certain
phrases like tho following, *sacred table, sacred and august
temple, sacred ceremony, holy sacraments, sacred traditions, etc.,* all words and usages not Christian, but simply papistical. And than those bare-footed friars of the
Valleys used to meet round the *table* of the refectory to
dine, and then talk of church matters, as did the monks
of the Middle Ages; baving become Protestants they
perhaps continued the enstom: only that the *table* whore
they used to take food became a place of meeting
for them, whenco the institution of tho *Waldensian*

Table, a kind of ecclesiastical government of that Church, and presided over by a *Moderator*, perhaps to moderate them, when the reverend gentlemen quarrel in their stormy Synods.

The Waldenses were the real and first *Protestants* who always continued to protest *in certain things* against Rome, and that up to our own times. He who supposes them to be the descendants of Christians persecuted under the emperors Decius and Diocletian, is in the wrong: the Waldenses were Romanists and the history of their protests begins in the XII century (1). The greater part of the errors brought into the Roman Church from the death of the Apostles until the year 1000 were introduced among them, and are still jealously retained by the Waldenses. The greater part of the usages, of the Jewish ceremonies, and of the traditions of the Romanists had been already sanctioned and recognized by the Waldensian friars before they separated from Rome; and when they forsook her, they retained all that Rome had previously invented, with the exception of the celibacy of the priests, idolatry and purgatory.

.

(1) " The Waldenses do not appear till the end of the XII " century: Alphonso II, King of Arragon calls them thus in " a decree which he made against them " (De Potter, *Stor. del Crist* § 2 p. 402 et seq. Turin. 1856).

II.

SLAUGHTER OF THE WALDENSES BY THE CATHOLICS.
AND OF THE CATHOLICS BY THE WALDENSES.

Since 1100, the Waldenses, shut up in the farthest
corner of the Alps which separate Italy from France,
more French than Italian, (their language, their customs
and their French names provo it) were able to oppose
themselves to the later innovations of Rome, and to
resist her still. Peter Damiano reproached the Countess
of Savoy, but in vain, for the Waldenses immediately
sent missionaries into Italy, so that Otto IV commanded
the archbishop of Turin to send them away (*Gioffredo
St. delle Alpi Marit. in Monum. hist. pat. t.* III, *p.* 784).
But their missions were continued in Lombardy, in
Tuscany, in Switzerland and in Upper Germany (*Hist.
of the Helvetic conf. p.* 179, 189; *Mem. hist. t.* I, *p.* 64).
Afterwards they were strengthened by Peter Waldo,
who gave them the name of Waldenses, which they bear
in our own days.

Finally the Church of Rome had recourse to the secu-
lar arm, and invented the Inquisition in order to destroy
heresy. The flames, the scaffold and the axe cut down
the Christians in France, in Germany, in Spain, in Italy;
the Waldenses remained. The emperor Frederick II,
pope Honorius III, and Innocent VIII, also a pope,
thundered forth sentences of death against them and
proclaimed a crusade. But the Waldenses, not unlike St.
Dominic, who, singing psalms, slaughtered the heretics,

3

also singing psalms, repulsed with great bloodshed « the arrogant and vile army » as says, with great propriety, a Waldensian historian! (Geymonat: *Gli Evang. Vald.* p. 29). See the contrary in the Bible, so often falsely quoted as to be blasphemed by infidels; (Prov. xxiv, 29; Matt. v, 38, 39; Rom. xii, 17, 19; 1 Cor. vi, 7; 1 Thess. v, 15; I Pet. iii, 9; Rev. xiii, 10), and as to the wrong application of the Scriptures 2 Pet. iii, 16. — From the xiii to the xv century, they resumed their missions in Provence, and sent some into Calabria. A certain Baron d'Oppède, general of Francis I of France, persecuted them ferociously in 1540; and Berosus, in the pay of Charles III of Savoy, oppressed them at the same time. Then followed years of blood and massacre on the part of the Catholics against the Waldenses and on the part of the Waldenses against the Catholics, when those Protestants formed the « flying company of a hundred archers » guided by two pastors, who ought to have moderated the impetuosity of the Waldensian assailants, but instead of this, the strife became most animated and sanguinary! — Then a Pianezza fell cruelly upon the mountaineers, and immediately afterwards Gianavelo and Giaiero, both Waldensians, fell cruelly upon the Catholics. It was a bitter, cruel war on both sides; this was in 1655. In the following year, a treaty of peace was signed at Pignerol. More massacres took place in 1661 on the blood-stained rocks of Angrogna, and after the revocation of the edict of Nantes, 1861, they began again with ferocity — each side being animated with such a destructive spirit as makes one shudder! Catinat destroyed many hundreds of them, and some .

Waldensians, says one of their historians (a minister of that Christ, who came to save, and not to lose, nor kill) « seeing them...... throw themselves with fury on the « garrison of that Commune, (Villar) surprise with won-« derful rapidity that of Torre, Luserna, S. Secondo, « with fire and sword spreading increasing panic and « terror » (Geymonat. *Gli Evang. Vald. p.* 65–69) and all this still in the name of the Lord! (Matt. xxvi, 52).

Next we see them exiled, then reconducted into the Valleys by the pastor Arnaud, who with the Bible in his left hand and the sword in his right, commanded them as their colonel; then they defeat the French at the bridge of Salabertrans in 1689, and encamp at Balsiglia. Here Arnaud first explained the word of grace and of forgiveness, then led the Waldenses to slaughter the Catholics, who, decimated and almost destroyed, retreat-ed, and the Waldenses reingratiated themselves with Victor Amadeus in 1690. And with this date terminate the sanguinary factions between the Catholics and the Waldenses, and we wish them never to be mentioned, but, seeing them now extolled by a too zealous Walder-sian, we cannot do otherwise than deplore them; — because if the Catholics can be justly reproached with intolerance and cruelty, impartial history can and ought also to reproach the Waldenses with violent actions, done, not with the Spirit of Grace, but with the Spirit of Abaddon (Rev. ix, 11). The Spirit of Grace, which is that of Jesus, does not enjoin a return to one's native country with the sword, but a retreat elsewhere; (Matt. x, 23) — does not say that our country is here, but that on earth we are strangers and foreigners (Eph. ii,

19); — does not tell us to kill those who wish to kill us, but proclaims that they who have taken the sword shall perish by the sword (Matt. xxvi, 52; Gen. iv, 6; Rev. xiii, 10); — and adds: revenge not yourselves, but give place unto wrath (Rom. xii, 19); and that Christ when he was reviled, reviled not again, but committed himself to Him who judgeth righteously (1 Pet. ii, 23). If, however, the Old Testament be quoted to justify war, violence and slaughter, as is done by the Roman Catholics and as did Dominic de Guzman, we answer that this confounds the Law with Grace, the economy of God as Sovereign of his people, with the economy of Grace, in which Christ says on the Cross: « Father, forgive them, for they know not what they do » (Luke xxiii, 34). And we repeat again, that it would be no better than the inquisitors, who singing and quoting psalms and passages from the Old Testament, and not from the New, slew to the glory of God! We wish to suppose that in our days the Waldenses would not act like their bellicose ancestors, otherwise the Gospel which renders us *sheep for the slaughter* (Rom. viii, 36) would be a *lying* word in their mouth!

III.

THE WALDENSES UP TO THE PRESENT TIME.

The historical sketch which we have traced shows that the Waldenses were the true Protestants, because the first to oppose themselves to Rome, when, already corrupt and idolatrous in the X century, she apostatized entirely from the Gospel. Their Church, persecuted by the Papists, met bloodshed with bloodshed, force with force; — banished, she regained her country with arms in her hands, and although her history may be glorious according to man and to human rights, it is not a very Christian history.

The Waldenses existed still through many centuries. but their faith and their testimony became more and more weak, superficial, traditional. Truly it appears that all those Churches which have shed blood have been judicially punished by God, and have no life at all, however they may struggle to show some; thus the Greek Church is blood-stained through her schisms, the Roman Church is stained with the blood of the martyrs, the Waldensian Church is stained by her violent repulses and by the slaughter of the Catholics. Oh yes! the Church which has shed blood has a name that she liveth, but is dead (Rev. III, 1). And in fact what is the Waldensian religion in these days? It is a form, a ceremonial of Sundays and of traditions; — and the Gospel which is life, is to the Waldensians a book of morality, while atheism and vice inundate their native valleys. Felix Neff of Geneva, a Protestant minister who visited them in 1821, was disheartened, and considered the Waldensian Church to be dying, if not dead. In fact, rationalism had penetrated therein, and the ministers were either ignorant, or obliged to study in Protestant countries beyond the Alps, and brought back the doctrines of the different schools in which they had studied theology.

The Waldensians of the present day are no longer

those of old, but are embellished Protestants. Those meditated upon the Word of God day and night (1); these
puzzle their brains about ecclesiastical history, traditions,
morals, and theology, which now is full of mere rationalism, the great heresy of the XIX century first given
us by Kant, and then nourished and become colossal
in Protestant Germany. Emancipated by Charles Albert
and recognized as the National Church of the Waldensian Valleys, they descended into Italy to protestantize
her in the name of the Gospel. Without a knowledge
of Italian habits and customs, without the power of
speaking our language correctly, they began to preach,
not the Church of Christ, but the Waldensian Church, not
the Gospel, but their Constitution, not the union of believers in Jesus, but the union of those who gave their names
to the registrars of the parishes; and that too without
having unity even among the ministers, for here was heard
salvation by grace, there a professor of theology taught
salvation also by works (Geymonat: *Difesa della dot-*
trina evangelica, p. 9), elsewhere evangelical morals (we
know not what this means, since Christ speaks of eternal
life). And then the pastors assembled yearly in the Valleys
sometimes offer to the Christian world the strange and
scandalous spectacle of their stormy synods. And many
of them leave the Valleys in a most deplorable spiritual state, and the Waldensians exposed to the snares
of the Mormons and of the Irvingites, who make converts, and of the Catholics, who have lately opened pro-
pagand schools — yet they leave the Valleys and go into

(1) De Potter. l. c. p. 404.

Italy to preach that Christ, of whom Paul speaks in Philipp. 1. 15 and 16.

IV.

THE REFORMATION OF THE XVI CENTURY.

In the XVI century the innovations, the violence and the corruptions of Romanism had arrived at such a point that no one believed any thing; credulity and incredulity were the results of ignorance on one side and civilization on the other, when God sounded forth a call, which, although through the work of man it may not have been in all its principles entirely pure and spiritual, nevertheless He intended to place the Bible in the hands of men, and He did so. Since that time Ho has been calling to all sinners, « Search the Scriptures » (John v, 39). « Verily, verily, I say unto you, He that heareth my word, and believeth on him that sent me, hath everlasting life, and shall not come into condemnation; but is passed from death unto life « (John v, 14). »

This is how the Protestant Reformation began:

Pope Leo X having become an earthly king, filled Europe with blood, exciting princes against princes; and having also hired soldiers himself, he robbed the Signore della Rovere of the Duchy of Urbino, placed and established his own family in Tuscany, tried to take Parma and Placentia, and in union with the Spaniards, desolated the Milanese. Meanwhile he collected artists, buffoons and comedians at Rome, and gave himself up to pleasures; and to get money for such things and also for

completing the building of St. Peter's, he published the
bulls of indulgences. Martin Luther, an Augustine friar
rose against those bulls, began to preach courageously
against the Pope, promulgated the reformation of the
Church, recanted, then returned to the attack with greater
force (1517 to 1520) and drew after himself the people,
princes and learned men. Meanwhile John Calvin was
doing the same in Switzerland, Cranmer in England,
and John Knox in Scotland. But it was a *Reformation
of the Romish Church* made by man, and not an *innova-
tion* performed by God, (2 Cor. v, 17; Rom. vɪɪɪ, 9;
Gal. vɪ, 15) therefore its authors felt themselves grow
weak, were not supported *by faith in the Lord*, but leant,
as Romanism had done, upon the princes of this world.
Thus the Reformation became worldly from its birth,
threw confusion into people's consciences, and produced
eclecticism.

The reformation had its followers and its martyrs in
Italy, but the persecutions of the Popes, aided by the
princes of those violent times, destroyed it by means of
slaughter, of exile and the stake. It took firm root in
freer countries, but the Reformation having arisen all
at once, without a true and profound knowledge of the
Word, necessarily took forms and doctrines which are
not in the Scriptures, but rather in former religions, Ju-
daism and Romanism. Notwithstanding this, the Reformers preached salvation by grace through faith, and
by this doctrine of life a great number of their followers
were saved. But not by Protestant principles and forms.
The want of knowledge of the Scriptures, and the violent introduction of Jewish and Romish forms into the

Church generated among them errors and sects from the very beginning. But that which is worse, even up to the present time, the *form* was always more powerful to them than the *spirit*, and they tore each other continually to save the former, not the latter; and thus, instead of charity in one and the same faith, for which they broke loose from Rome, they retained certainly one faith, so that their Church may be called one, but their sects multiplied, became jealous, bitter against each other, turned their backs on each other, and refused to unite and to love one another. This constitutes their greatest sin, because it is Jesus Christ who saves, unites and sanctifies, and we are neither saved, nor are we believers through any Church denomination whatever.

V.

OF THE PRINCIPAL PROTESTANT CHURCHES.
SUMMARY OF THEIR ERRORS.

The Anglicans, the Lutherans, the Calvinists are national protestants, sometimes having a clerical hierarchy, sometimes not, but all having a liturgy which replaces, as in the Romish Church, the worship of the Spirit. The Waldenses are in this group of protestants, being in part maintained by the state (Geymonat. p. 89) and retaining in their Church all, good or bad, who are born in the Valleys of Piedmont. They have a liturgy like the Romanists, a confession of faith which is not pure, and not to be proved by the Word; they are governed, as we have said in the beginning of this chapter, by a

presbyterian *table* like the Protestants of Scotland, and
have parishes, like the priests, for their congregations
(*V. Constit chap.* 1).

The Free Church of Scotland, the Baptists, the
Wesleyans and Dissenters in general are not national
Protestants, because not paid by the government, but
they all retain the same clericalism which separates ministers from laymen: — sometimes they have liturgies,
sometimes not, — and more or less in their nominal liberty and their warm disagreements, they elevate their
principle into that of a clearly defined sect. They *err*:

1. In proclaiming that their liberty consists in al-
lowing any one to be a member of their congregations
on his own responsability, and thus they permit the
hypocrite to enter for social convenience and without
the « right hand of fellowship » (Gal. ii, 9; Acts ii, 47)
of the other members.

2. In holding that baptism is the point of union,
and not faith, which binds us to Christ and to his
people. (Heb. xi, 6; Rom. v, 1; Eph. ii, 8; iii, 12) (1)

3. That without perfection, the believer cannot be
saved, forgetting that we ought to have that which is
imputed to us from Christ and not that which flesh may
give us (Rom. viii, 29, 30; vii, 18).

Then in general all Protestants have a quantity of
errors; we will point out the principal of them, as we

(1) Here it is right to observe that the Waldenses did not
baptize infants in the first period of their separation from
Rome. « Their baptism consisted in ablutions alone, and they
only conferred it upon adults. » (De Potter. *Stor. del Crist.* ¿. 2.
p. 404).

have hitherto done, and as we shall always do, by appeal
to the Word of God, which says the contrary. Protestants then,

1. *Err* in having fixed their religion as a national
one, while the religion of Christ is only for *believers*:
« He that believeth on me hath eternal life » says Jesus
(John VI, 47). « He that believeth and is baptized shall
be saved; » (Mark XVI, 16) where is the nationality? if
He adds, he that believeth not shall he condemned!
(March XVI, 16 John. III, 18). Are all those who com-
pose a Protestant nation believers? Alas! the answer
might be dreadful!

2. *Err* in having made of the ministers a caste, as
the Church of Rome had done, a priesthood which separates itself from the rest of the faithful, whilst all believers have duties and rights according to the gift of
God; all are members one of another, Jesus being the
head of the body (Eph II, 18, 22; 1 Cor. XII, XIII, XIV;
Heb. XIII, 15; 1 Piet, II, 4, 9). (1)

3. They *err* in fixing a liturgy, like and in the
manner of the Church of Rome, or like the little devo-
tional books of the Catholics, and thus they quench the
Spirit in the assembly. By the Spirit and not by the
liturgy is given the « word of wisdom, » the « word of
knowledge; » (1 Cor. XII) by the Spirit and not by the
liturgy prayer is offered (Rom. VIII, 26, 27; Eph. VI,
18, ec).

(1) Once the Waldenses had the priesthood more diffused
in the Church and more Christian. De Potter says (p. 404) « To
sum up, the priesthood belonged to every upright man » among
them.

4. *They err* very often, not in the doctrines which are fundamental to salvation, but necessary to faithfulness, as in baptisms, baptizing infants as in the Romish Church, and against the Word, which will *only* have *believers* baptized (March xvi, 16).

5. *They err* in the Lord's supper, giving the bread cut into small pieces, as the priest gives the wafer, and against the Word, which says that we ought *to break it* (1 Cor. x, 16; Acts xx, 7; ii, 42).

6. *They err* in having the Lord's supper administered by a minister, as does the Romish Church, and in not permitting any believer to give thanks and break the bread, according to the custom of the primitive Christians. (Acts ii, 46; xx, 7).

7. *They err* in performing marriages which God in Heaven binds, and not the priest or the minister; and in attributing to themselves the civil power, which merely recognizes the two whom God has already united. (Mark x, 9). They will not find one verse in the Bible, which justifies such usurped authority.

8. *They err* in burying the dead, using pagan ceremonies, and not the primitive simplicity (Act. viii, 2).

9. *They err* in the imposition of hands, which at first was only a sign of the gift already received, (Acts xiii, 3; 1 Tim. iv, 14) and now they pretend that it is an act to give power to administer the *sacraments* (?), which word is not found in the Bible, but in the Roman traditions.

10 *They err* when any one of these sects pretends to be the true Church. The true Church is in God our Father and in the Lord Jesus Christ (1 Thes i, 1).

VI.

OF THE CONGREGATIONS OF THE « BRETHREN. »

There are in England, in France, in Germany, and in Switzerland other meetings of the faithful who assemble in the name of the Lord, all possessing the same faith in Jesus the Saviour, and exercising one discipline. Many of them have a free ministry in the Church, like some congregations of dissenters in Germany, England and Switzerland. But they retain a special ministry to break the bread, and thus they also have a clerical principle, not provoable by the Word. Only the Plymoutbists, (Christians who met together at first in Plymouth in England, whence they had this name), and the Darby-ists, (the followers of J. N. Darby), saw that they could not preserve that ministry because it was not scriptural, and having abandoned it, they assemble in liberty and simplicity according to the Gospel. These two bodies were at first a single one, but the spirit of division came into the midst of the brethren and they were divided by Darby, who with his adherents separated himself, falsely accusing the Plymonthists of tolerating the er-rors of Newton, whom *both* had rejected from amongst them. The followers of Darby retained a sectarian disci-pline, by which they exclude from the Lord's supper Christians who do not think with them; they often even excommunicate whole assemblies of Christians! It is a lay papistry and nothing else! — With these their sec-tarian principles they did and still do harm in England,

and naturally caused a commotion in the Churches on the continent, especially in France and Switzerland. Their aim is not to preach repentance and conversion of sinners to Jesus Christ, but to enter every where into works already established and done without them, and they enter in order to cast into their midst the English discords, to embitter hearts, disunite them one from the other, instil into them a spirit of continual murmuring, of rash judgements, of feigned charity, and to divide the Churches into two parties, one of which goes over to them only to return shortly to that from which it had separated itself! Sad occupation, mournful story!

The Plymouthists remained in simplicity, but being too jealous of the equality of the brethren, are rather too intractable in recognizing ministers and in obeying the leaders (Heb. xiii, 17; 1 Thess. v, 12, 13; Phil. ii, 25, 29).

These two rocks on which the English brethren have split will be avoided, it is to be hoped, by the Italians. Up to the present time they have indeed avoided them, because they have walked according to the Word, and in all the free Churches of Italy there are ministers who conduct, without hindrance to the gifts of the Spirit in the other brethren.

CHAPTER III.

THE CHRISTIAN CHURCH.

~~~~~~

I.

THE REFORMERS AND THE CHRISTIANS IN ITALY.

Our Italy had in every age Reformers of the Romish
Church, and Christians according to the Gospel.

The Italian Reformers were nearly all ex-priests and
ex-monks, with a few men illustrious by their learning
or their birth, who were adverse to the Pope and his
dogmas, not for the love of Christ, but to give a better
position to Italy. They began with Arnaldo da Brescia,
and have continued to our own days, with the canon
Reali, Padre Passaglia, Liverani and the monk A. Gavazzi. Some more and some less believed, and still
believe, that it is necessary to reform and not to inno-
vate, that the Pope ought to be a simple bishop and not
a temporal prince; that politics ought not to be separated from religion, that in the Church there ought to be
a caste of priests and a flock of laymen; that the primitive traditions ought to be retained with the Gospel;

that believers should see themselves registered not in the
« book of life » which is in heaven, bnt in tho book of
the parish; that it is necessary to have members, no
matter of what sort of pernous, whether believers, hypo-
crites or dissolute people, and that the ex-Romish priest
who goes to minister among them ought to bo chief
pastor, and every thing, in fact a pope in XVIII^mo. Their
evangelization is that of philosophers, of politicians, of
learned men, and a continual controversy against the
Church of Rome, and against the political government
of the people, — for, despots and priests more than the
Pope himself in their reformed Churches, they nevertheless wish to play the democrat in society! The fathers
of this Church, (not that they ever ministered in it, hnt
being so much invoked and quoted by them, we also
will note them here) are Abelard, Arnaldo da Breccia,
Dante, Boccaccio, Petrarch, Lorenzo Valla, Poggio,
Bracciolini, the monk Battista da Mantova, the historian Guicciardini, (*Paralipomena ex autog. florent. re-
censita*, *p.* 46–48, *Amster.* 1663) Macchiavelli, Fra
Paolo Sarpi, Fra Benedetto Foiano, Cecco d'Ascoli, Ni-
cola Franco, Giordano Bruno, Fra Girolamo Savonarola,
Egidio Viterbo, Gian Francesco Pico della Mirandola,
and Ugo Bassi. The neo–Catholics and neo–Christians,
who follow this school are (some more, some less,) conscientious and honest in the object at which they aim;
some with a measure of faith in Christ, but saturated
with politics and democracy, others tending either to
reform the Romish Church, or to erect a Church which
resembles her under another name. We will not speak
of these reformers who were not, are not, nor ever will

be the Christian Church in Italy, whatever may be the clamour they may succeed in raising, now or hereafter, in this poor Italy of ours, and whatever name they may assume. We will speak instead of the Christians, who witnessed for Jesus Christ at the time of the Reformation, and who, although they were friends of the foreign Reformers, had little or nothing to do with them.

Without protestantizing in the manner of the foreigners, those Italians of the XVI century, who met simply to read and meditate on the Word, showed a living faith in Christ, receiving from Christ indeed so strong a faith that they witnessed for it by martyrdom. In Ferrara they gathered round Celio Secundo Curione, Marcantonio Flaminio, and Pellegrino and Olimpia Marata. Many were the assemblies of the brethren in Ferrara in 1528 and at Modena there were also some, God having there made use of the Sicilian Paolo Ricci, known by the name of Lisias Fileno, and that in 1540. In 1525, the Gospel penetrated into Tuscany, where Carnesecchi and Martire began to witness for it; and into Siena, where were then Aonio Palcario, author of the « Beneficio della morto di Cristo, » and Ochinus, who afterwards made shipwreck of the faith. In Pisa, in 1543, many converts to the Gospel broke bread together. In Lucca, Martire evangelized, and Paolo Lancisio, Celso Martinengo, Emanuele Treniellys. In Naples many Christians were gathered round Don Giovanni Valdes, the secretary of the Viceroy Galeazzo Caraccioli, Francesco Caserta, Pier Carnesecchi, Vittoria Colonna, Giulia Gonzaga. At Bologna, Giovanni Moltio di Montalcino preached the Gospel, and Bucero, in a letter dated

4

1541, says there were many Christians there. Battista da Crema preached in the Lombard states in 1536, Baldassare Fontana and Benedetto Locarno in the city of Locarno, Balbo Supertino, Baldassare Altieri and Carnesecchi in Venice, Pier Paolo and Giovan Battista Vergerio in Istria, and many others, who certainly were in relation with some of the Reformers, but neither for money, through vanity, nor through ignorance did they allow themselves to be corrupted by them so as to adopt their practices; this is why their faith was a living one and accompanied them to their martyrdom. It would suffice to read some letters of Pier Paolo Vergerio, who, a faithful preacher of the Gospel, laments over « Lutheranism, » which further on he calls « Saxon merchandise, » as a thing which « grieves him. » (*letter to Ottonello Vida*).

Of the noble list of confessors of Jesus Christ which we have traced, many sealed their faith with their blood, others languished in the prisons of the Inquisition, others fled or were driven into exile, but very few of them embraced the ideas of Protestants on the hierarchy, on ceremonies, and on traditions. They set an example to us Italians, and if we are *truly and sincerely Christ's*, we shall imitate them.

II.

Now we will give a very rapid summary of the history of the religious revival effected by God in Italy in the present century.

It began by the will of God in Tuscany, where the Lord silently opened the hearts of several persons, converted them to himself and put in them the desire to testify to others the grace which they had received from Him. During the political revolution from 1847 to 1849 the Christians of Tuscany took advantage of that liberty to announce the Gospel more openly, and the converts were many; they met together in simplicity, meditated upon the Word of God, and broke bread; but after the restoration of despotism they were watched, persecuted, then threatened, then imprisoned, and finally driven into banishment. Three of them fixed themselves in Piedmont. — There they became better acquainted with the Waldenses, but they did not join that Church. They were jealous of the spiritual priesthood and the ministry, which they had found in the Word (1 Pet. II. 9). And they would not resign it, — jealous of the freedom of « breaking bread » as it is written in the Word (Acts II, 46) — jealous of the precious gift of making known Jesus Christ and Him crucified, for which they had been driven into exile, and they wished to use it like those « who were scattered abroad » after the death of Stephen. (Acts viii, 4). — They were afraid of priests and ex-priests, it mattered little whether Romanist or Protestant, but nearly all without life, without orthodoxy, and full of pride and vanity.

While the Tuscans were testifying of Jesus Christ, and they who felt the necessity of believing in the Lord met together in their houses, the Waldenses were writing to England, to Scotland, Switzerland, Holland and America for money, received it in abundance, built temples, and made a great stir. But it did not last long — because the Florentine refugees, who exiled for the testimony of Jesus, amid many corruptions and troubles preserved the purity of Christian principles — already had a crowd of hearers, already many converts met with them in simplicity. And this without noise and the vanity of *reports*. The Lord blessed immensely the faithfulness of the Italian Church, which appeared then in Piedmont full of life and light. From among her members came forth workmen and artisans, unlettered in the history of controversy and of theology, but full of courage and of the gift of evangelization, who went out into the other subalpine cities to preach the Gospel. Crowds of people eagerly listened to the words of the evangelists, who visibly showed that God had sent them. By their instrumentality arose other faithful Churches which live by Divine life, in which other artisans and workmen minister — where the Gospel is announced in purity, — where the faithful break bread on the first day of the week.

III.

Whilst God was endowing the Italian Church with the gift of evangelization — continued — incessant — active, — there arose by her side works of contention.

The first were the Waldenses.

The Waldenses had already had the proof that Protestantism does not become fruitful in this soil. They knew that God had given to the Italians a clear conception of things, and that if it were proposed to them to conform to a religion which has a constitution, a liturgy, Romish festivals (as Easter, Christmas, New Year's day, Ascension, Good Friday, *Costit. Vald. Cap.* VIII) fasts, clergy and laity, they would answer with great soundness of judgement: we have all these things with the Pope of Rome, and certainly we will not leave them off in order to embrace others, modelled upon the popish pattern. — They knew that if the pure Gospel just as it is written, *without a tradition, a custom whatever*, were offered to the Italians, they would embrace Jesus Christ. And not to do thus, as God wishes, is a great sin. — They knew that the momentary crowds in their Churches in Italy were the effect of curiosity, and that they always ended in the total desertion of all, and in atheism produced by a doctrine which is not pure. — They knew that their Temples were frequented (as soon as the fickle crowds have disappeared) by Waldensians

who speak French and by foreign Protestants, and not
by Italians. — They knew that they preach in Italian
to foreigners who do not understand our language, only
to make it believed that they are doing a work in Italy;
and yet the Waldensians ministers, turning their backs
on their Valleys and on their compatriots, who, like
the Ninevites « cannot discern between their right hand
and their left, » (Jonah IV. 11), (and one must go and
live there a while in order to see with one's own eyes),
led astray by the Catholics who are in the midst of them
and with whom they associate in holiday-making, in
dancing, and in vice, without having gained one prose-
lyte, but vice versa, — the Waldenses would follow the
Italians and evangelize by their side, in order to disturb the work of God which is to be performed by
Italians, and not by foreigners who preach their own
forms, their own creeds, their own priests, and not
purely and simply « Christ and Him crucified. »

Oh! conscientious history will one day tell how,
when the Waldenses came from Piedmont, they were
unable to effect any stable or true work through our
aversion to priestcraft, to popes, and to Protestantism.
It will tell how from the beginning the Waldensians
have been the most tenacious and the most tiresome ad-
versaries of the Italian Church, and that the Christians of
Italy have not suffered from the Papists the half of that
which they have endured from the Waldenses. It will tell
how the Waldenses come between Christians, as do the
Darbyists in France and in Switzerland, and say first that
their Church is the same as the Italian one, then they
defame the latter, and to wheedle and seduce simple

minds they add that they are approved by Government,
— that they have money with which to help the poor,
because oltramontane Protestants provide them with it
abundantly; and thus they seek to bewitch, to foment
discords and to sow scandals. — It will say how many
falsehoods have been printed by the Waldenses against
the Christian Church in Italy in the newspapers of
Scotland and of Paris, in their own « Buona Novella, »
etc. etc. — It will say that the Christian Church did not
trouble itself about the falsehoods of others, and has
preferred that judgement should come from God. — It
will say that it, exposed to the continuous efforts of the
Waldenses, and of all the clericals of the earth, has res-
isted, and still resists, by the Divine strength. — These
and other things will history relate, if true and conscientious history be ever written in Italy; in any case
we are certain that these and other things, which we
omit through Christian charity, will appear *as we have
said them* in the day of the « *revelation of the righteous
judgement of God.* (Rom. II, 5).

IV.

WORK OF THE PROTESTANT CHURCHES IN ITALY.

Another fact which *true* and not *party history* will
make clear some day is, that the beautiful and holy testimony rendered to the Lord by the Italian Christians
drew into this country of ours. one by one, all the other
foreign sects who sought to seduce the brethren in or-

der to draw them, each sect to itself. A work, we hardly know whether to call more puerile or more wicked! But the priests of the Reformation made no scruple about the matter, and continued and still continue this work of dissolution, giving to Italy the strange spectacle of the Protestantism of a hundred sects, of a hundred confessions of faith; all of them priests, and neither more nor less intolerant than Rome. And yet they speak of working for the glory of God !

Therefore besides the Italian Church we have in Italy :

1. The *Waldensian Church*, of which we have spoken above.

2. The *Scotch Church*. It has presbyteries like the Waldenses, but, amongst all the Protestant communions, the Scotch are those who approach most nearly to the ministry of the Church according to the Gospel — they break the bread instead of receiving it from the minister in tiny morsels as do the Waldenses — and they have an order of worship, not a liturgy. And yet the Scotch, such jealous maintainers of their own doctrines and of their Church forms, are those who keep side by side with the Waldenses, aid and support them, and *will* not see that the Italians *absolutely refuse to Waldensianize themselves*. It is said that they have become one body at Naples, but they will soon be like the Waldensians in Piedmont and in Tuscany, that is, with congregations composed of their Waldensian countrymen, of foreigners living in or passing through the city, with a few ignorant or vain Italians — the « coryphées » of their « Temples. »

3. The *Anglican Church*. The English who belong to
this Church made many attempts to establish a national Church in Italy after the pattern of the Church
of England. They never succeeded, nor do they try
any longer. And here we may be permitted to give
due praise to them, for as soon as they perceived
that the Italians wished for the preaching of the Gospel
and nothing else — they did not weaken the hearts of
believers by clerical disputes, they imposed nothing,
they ordered nothing, but, proposing to advance the
glory of God, they encouraged the Italians to preach
Jesus Christ and Him crucified. It must be owned that
the spirit of this Church is a Christian one, and the love
which it has for the preaching of the Gospel is sincere,
without any idea of imposing the forms of the Anglican Church. In England too it is the only Church which
encourages the religious movement without minding
forms and creeds; it is the only Church which does not
look with an evil eye upon the layman, who, without
having received the imposition of hands, preaches the
Word — it is the only Church which looked affection-
ately upon the late religious revival — it is the only
Church which has produced those publishers of the Gospel, from amongst the people, the middle classes, and
the nobility, who, in the power of the Spirit, announce
salvation by grace through faith. We are glad to render
this tribute to the English Church — without however
belonging to it — and we grieve that the other Churches, from a sectarian and priestly spirit, do not merit
it, as they are working in contention and vainglory.

4 The *Irvingite Church*. It recruits a few proselytes

among the Waldensians in the Valleys of Piedmont, and among the ex–Romish priests, but for some years has done no more, nor can do, with its errors, its superstitions and its clericalism.

5. The *Methodists or Wesleyans*, with their strange doctrine of perfection, with their sighs, and with an exterior which may take in some Christians, who are weak or ignorant of the Word. They move about Florence, Milan, Naples — slip in every where with a smiling face and hands full of gold to buy unstable souls and vain men, and go every where to recruit proselytes in the strength of the God Mammon. They penetrate into the meetings to try the Christians, to test the faith of the evangelists, offering them money, and busy themselves in opening schools to draw people to Methodism. It is true that the Italians are too much averse to priests to bend under the yolk of Methodist priests; — it is true that we esteem too highly the dignity of the Italian name to believe that our fellow-countrymen will welcome this foreign sect for a little gold, or from vanity; it is true also that the Methodists publish as with sound of trumpet that they do not instruct the evangelists to preach Methodism, but certain facts, which they know well, might prove them in the wrong: — in any way it is right that the Italians may know — having escaped from the *methodism* of the priests of Rome — how not to fall into *that* of the Methodist or Wesleyan priests, — for one sect is as good as the other.

6. *The followers of the monk Gavazzi.* It is to be lamented that Gavazzi should not always preach Christ

and Him crucified, but a mixture of politics and religion. Certainly the Gospel does not make us cease to be citizens, but it appears to us that the pulpit of the truth ought not to be that of politics or of polemics; *there* the Word of God is addressed to *souls* that are saved or to be saved by Jesus. If one goes to the bottom of his intention it seems that Gavazzi wants a *reformation* (not a making all new, according to the Gospel), a *Creed*, (not that which consists *in the whole* Bible) a *catechism* to make believers according to a new Church: the *primitive, evangelical Church of the Apostle Paul*, (1) a *numerous Church and inscribed in the register*, a presbyterian pastorate to direct the Church — which is not a little surprising, because Gavazzi who is democratic. appears despotic in clerical forms! And yet he knows that priestcraft is the *sole* and *true* ruin of the Christian faith; nor can Gavazzi believe the Protestant priests to be much better than the priests of Rome. — It is true that the priests and monks who come away from Rome, democratic or not, gifted by God or not, do not know how to take the humble post of *servant* in the Christian Church, but wish to rule and direct her, with what wis-

(1) We do not understand what Gavazzi means: 1, because the N. Test. speaks of the *Christian Ch.* (Acts. xi, 26; xxvi, 28; 1 Pet. iv, 16) and not of the *Evangelical Ch* (a name which comes to us from the Prussian Churches); 2, because the Ch. of Christ has not only the Word of the Gospels, but also that of the Epistles and all the Scriptures (Eph. :1, 26; 2 Pet. iii, 2); 3, because the Word speaks of the *Church of Christ* (Eph. i, 22. 23), not of the *Church of Paul*, for the simple reason that it is not the body of Paul, but the body of Christ.

dom alas! we know too well. But it is also true that the
Italians want neither priests nor reverends; but the Bible, the whole Bible, and nothing but the Bible.

Finally it is right to declare in order to avoid all
equivocation, that these communions of Protestants have
nothing to do with the Christian Church in Italy.

V.

PRINCIPLES OF THE CHRISTIAN CHURCH.

In the face of this Babel of sects which come to us
from beyond mountains and beyond seas, the Christian
Church, arisen in Italy amidst persecutions and grown
up in sufferings, perseveres and continues to contend
for the faith which was once delivered to the saints
(Jude 3). As it has been already observed, she only
wants the Bible, without fathers, without traditions,
without theology. — It is true that many Protestant
priests call us false names, to vituperate us and expose
us to the derision of their companions and of the Catholics, just as the unbelieving Jews called the disciples of
Jesus sectarians, Galileans, and Nazarenes, but as those
very ancient brothers of ours did not care for priests and
evil speakers, and continued in the way of the Lord, so
we will not trouble ourselves in the least. And do not
believe that we do this from a party spirit, no, but for
love of peace. For we really desire to live in communion
with all who in sincerity of heart invoke the name of
the Lord, but when, from sectarian feeling, the priests
of every name come to disturb us in order to impose

upon us their decaying forms which are worn threadbare
in their own countries, and which are the cause of the
rationalism and the infidelity of their nations, then the
Lord commands us to depart from them (Rev. XVIII. 4;
2 Cor. VI, 14–18).

Certainly faith in the Lord Jesus ought to unite all
Christians, and this is our mind on the subject of receiving joyfully Christians *of all denominations*, but not the
dissolute or the unbelieving; but when we see the
priests of the Reformation leave this work of charity, and
come amongst us to lead the brethren astray, defame
them by means of the press, and recommend their own
forms and their own priests (in this century that wants
neither forms nor priests, which are the cause of all un-
belief), deep grief oppresses us! *For some of these*, of
whom alone we speak, the form is all, the life nothing
— the priest or the minister is all, the believer nothing —
theology is all, the Bible nothing — an empty and ra-
tionalistic phraseology is all, the Holy Spirit nothing.
And as the papist finds religion where there are saints,
the mass, and a pulpit, so the Protestant priest says
that religion is to be found where there are reformed
priests, a liturgy, traditions, and a pulpit; if instead of
these monkish dirges they find in an assembly the supper of the Lord amongst believers, prayers not read but
dictated from a regenerate heart, which feels and speaks
by the Holy Spirit, a seat or a bench instead of a pulpit, and a layman or a workman who preaches the Gospel instead of a man in a gown or a white cravat, they
exclaim « disorder! » And in like manner would they
probably have exclaimed in the first days of Christianity.

when poor fishermen, with hardened hands, without a gown, devoid of theology, of science and of grammar, put to shame the arrogance of the learned men of Judea, of Greece, and of the Roman empire (1 Cor. i, 27, 28). We shall have life so long as we see men of the lower orders, and plebeians, endowed by God, announcing with power and with simplicity the Gospel of Grace;— but when we see forms, clericalism, priestly vanity in the churches, the clericals may indeed cry — now we have order in the churches — and with their empty voices they may fill journals, circulars, and the whole world, to receive the reward spoken of by Christ in Matthew vi. 2, 5, — but in them, and amongst them there will be neither life, nor love, nor brotherhood, and they will exactly resemble the Church of Sardis or that of Laodicea.

The principal things which the formalists wrongly impute to us, are the following:

1. *The want of a profession of faith.* They err, because we have one which is complete and most perfect: THE BIBLE. Beyond this we shall never have the boldness nor the folly to make another, because every confession of faith is maimed, incomplete, heretical and not pure, — because there always slip in traditions of the fathers which can form neither dogma nor doctrine. Add to which that every Creed or profession of faith must be *negative* and not *positive* for the reason that an extract of verses from the Bible is the negation of the others, or is not the positive and complete affirmation of all the Scriptures.

2. *The Lord's Supper every Sunday:* yes, we ob-

serve it on that day, because this was the practice of
the primitive Church. (Acts. II, 46; xx, 7). Can you
maintain from the Scriptures that it should be observed
only at Christmas and at Easter? — Can you prove that
the primitive Christians observed it only on those days?
— Can you even tell us exactly the day of the birth of
the Redeemer? — Can you, still from the Scriptures, prove that these two festivals are to be found in the
Gospel? — No, certainly. You have received them from
the Church of Rome, and we will have nothing popish
among us.

3. *The spiritual priesthood and the ministry of
saints:* we have, and are jealous of them, because Jesus
Christ has so constituted his Church (1 Cor. XII; 1
Pet. II, 5 etc.).

4. *The baptism of infants.* We do not baptize them.
because in no part of the Word is it written that it
should so be done: « He who believeth and is baptized
shall be saved », says Jesus Christ; now an infant cannot believe, as soon as it is born, therefore cannot be
baptized. Some will say: in baptism we offer the infant
to God — Is God Moloch or Saturn? And where is the
verse which authorizes you so to do?

5. *The want of an ecclesiastical form.* But if each
one of these clericals boasts of his particular form, and
maintains that it is the only true one — which of them.
we will ask, would be adapted to Italy? — Not one,
certainly: 1° because they are all, some more, some less,
popish and destructive of life; 2° because God has already constituted our Church, and has given us leaders,
evangelists, etc., but Protestants will not recognize

them, because God, instead of taking them out of their schools of theology, has taken them out of the Churches from amongst the people.

Oh Italians, believers in Jesus Christ! Let us leave those who have learnt little from the Word, from their own history, from their own people and from themselves, — and let us retain the organization of the Church which comes to us from God, — let us retain the Bible as our only rule of faith, as our model, our confession, our guide, our all; and if there be any one who from vanity or any other motive, complies with the requirements of the foreign sectarians and compromises the truth he has once known and taught, — let us pity him from the heart and pray to God for him.

VI.

THE PRACTICE OF THE CHURCH.

We believe that all the members of a meeting, redeemed by the blood of Jesus, have been made:

I. « Worshippers of God in spirit and in truth » (John. IV, 24).

II. « Kings and priests unto God his Father » (Rev. I, 6; 1 Pet. II, 5, 9).

And as such, every saved sinner can in the meeting:

I. *Confess the name of the Lord Jesus* (Rom. X. 9, 10).

II. *Pray*, (Rom. XII, 12; Col. IV, I; Eph. VI, 18; 1 Thess. V, 17).

III. *Give thanks* (Col. III, 17: Eph. V, 20; Heb. XIII, 15).

IV. *Break bread on the first day of the week* (Acts. xx, 7).

Therefore we cannot divide the meetings into two parts, that of the *clergy*, and that of the *laity*, as is admitted by Romish and Protestant priests. We cannot forbid a brother to confess the name of Jesus, to pray or give thanks. Nor can we receive the bread broken and in fractions from another, but we ought to break it, because it is written: « the bread which we break is it not the communion of the body of Christ? » (1 Cor. x, 16; Acts. xx, 7; II, 42).

In such an assembly, formed according to the Word, will be manifested and developed those gifts which God will bestow on some of his children for the edification of all, and thus « the whole body fitly joined together and compacted by that which every joint supplieth, according to the effectual working in the measure of every part, maketh increase of the body unto the edifying of itself in love » (Eph. iv, 16). And as we believe that God has given « some apostles and some prophets, » whose word is our foundation (Eph. ii, 20); so He gives and will give still « evangelists, pastors and teachers, for. the perfecting of the saints, for the work of the ministry, for the edifying of the body of Christ, till we all come in the unity of the faith, and of the knowledge of the Son of God, unto a perfect man, unto the measure of the stature of the fulness of Christ. » (Eph. iv, 11–13).

Now as it is written that « He has *given* » so we, if we mean to be faithful to the Word, ought to receive, not from men, nor from seminaries, nor schools of theo-

logy, evangelists, doctors, and pastors, but from God.
The duty of a meeting to which the Lord *gives* such
gifts is that of recognising them; not with any ceremony
or form whatever, nor clothed in a particular dress, —
but with a grateful heart, and with the feelings which the
Word enjoins to be shown to those who have the rule
over us (Heb. xiii, 17; 1 Thess. v, 12, 13). The ministry of the evangelist, of the pastor and of the doctor
does not nullify the collective and spiritual ministry of
the Church, nor ought that meeting which has a pastor.
a doctor, or an evangelist, to remain silent, and its
members cease to « confess the name of Jesus », to
« pray » and to « give thanks » in the public service.

The formalist Churches which live by ceremonies and
forms oppose us, saying that we reject the *laying on of
hands*. This form, a perfectly Jewish one, was used in
the primitive Church; — and in regard to the ministry.
not to *confer the gift* but to recognise it in those who
had already received it from God. In fact, hands were
laid upon Paul, who had already preached the Gospel
without having received the imposition of hands (Acts.
xiii, 3; Gal. i, 15–17). The passage in 1 Tim. v, 22, is
quoted, but Paul does not speak there of an apostolic
succession, nor of those who were afterwards to lay on
hands, as Papists and Protestants believe, but he exhorts
not to lay on hands hastily, as is done in the case of
those who, having passed through the schools of theology, are there and then made ministers by the laying
on of hands, and become afterwards carnal rationalists
and a shame to Christ. And besides, there being no
apostolic succession, from whom can the imposition of

hands be received? Where is Paul, and where is Timothy who might have performed it? We believe to be rash, or ignorant of the Word, all those who, followers of Rome or believing themselves to be Paul revived or Timothy risen again, *dare* to lay on hands! — Where is the verse which authorizes them to do so? Are they Paul or Timothy or Titus?

They usurp like the Papists an authority which they have not received from God.

We know from the New Testament that the Church ordained elders and deacons, when it felt the necessity of so doing (Acts. vi, 1-6), the first for the spiritual government of the Church, the others for material affairs, and these latter might also be evangelists (Acts xxi, 8). Although no one pretends now that the elders have gifts to communicate as in the apostolic times (1 Tim. iv, 14; Jam. v, 14-15), nevertheless we do not reject their ministry. Nearly all the Italian Churches recognise this ministry in some of their members, who exercise it in watching over the conduct and the morality of the Christians, in speaking at the Lord's Supper, in providing for the wants of the poor — and we equally recognise them, although Protestants reproach us with not having used any form in so doing. And it has been rather observed that in Italy, when an election has taken place with the vanity of carnal proceedings, the result has been deplorable, there not having been found in the elected the qualities required in the Word: 1 Tim. iii, 1-13; Titus i, 6, etc. It seems really as if God requires no forms, but only that the *gifts* which He *bestows* should be recognised.

Finally, the Christians of the Italian Church are all sinners saved by grace through faith (Eph. II, 8 9; Col. III, 12, 13,) having constant need of the blood of Christ « because in many things we offend all » (Jam. III, 2; 1 John. I, 8; II, 1, 2, etc.) and it is through the blood of Christ that they « have boldness to enter into the holiest » (Heb. x, 19).

They meet together frequently; they break bread on the first day of the week; their leaders preach the Gospel, teach, and the brethren edify one another.

They are persecuted, afflicted, calumniated. They want no Jewish and worldly forms, nor constitutions of reformed Churches, because Christ has already constituted the Church — nor the protection of the world, because they are not of the world (John. XVII, 16). They want no name except that of *Christians* through the grace of God (See Acts XI, 26; XXVI, 28; 1 Pet, IV. 16). They wish to be *Italians*, and not Waldensians, Scotch. nor Methodists, — they wish to be *Christians* and neither Papists, Protestants nor Reformed.

A Waldensian said in his little book: « *Novelties in religion are not progress.* » (Gli Evang. Vald. of P. Geymonat. p xv). Most precious truth! But when he adds « *let us all return to the religion of the Fathers* », we answer NO, because the so-called Fathers of every Church have deceived us more or less, and have destroyed the strength of the Word to make traditions and worldly forms triumph — therefore they deceive us who tell us to keep to the religion of the Fathers; — but we will rather say: *Let us all go to the religion of the Apostles, to the Gospel of the grace of God!*